Pope John Paul II was, without a doubt, a man of deep prayer. Cardinal Julian Herranz, who worked in the Roman curia for more than forty-five years, said that beyond the trips, the saint-making, and the media spectacles, there was another "first" about John Paul's pontificate that revealed who John Paul really was. No pope in recent times, Cardinal Herranz said, ever spent as much time in front of the tabernacle, where Catholics believe Christ is present in the form of consecrated bread, as did John Paul II.

People who had the chance to watch the Holy Father celebrate Mass in his private chapel remark about his reverence, his concentration, and his total absorption in the liturgy. The Eucharist was a font of faith that gave him the strength to carry on when his physical limits would have stopped most other men.

The Pope was also a strong advocate of private eucharistic adoration. He began a tradition of daily exposition of the Blessed Sacrament in St. Peter's Basilica. Upon the encouragement of Mother Teresa of Calcutta, he also opened a chapel for perpetual adoration in Rome.

This pamphlet is intended to help pass on to all readers a bit of the love and devotion Pope John Paul II had for our Lord in the Eucharist. Each topic is derived from his own writings. The accompanying prayers have been carefully selected with the hope that they will deepen the reader's love for God and promote greater devotion to the ancient and venerable practice of regular adoration of our Lord in the Eucharist.

God's Greatest Gift

Deep in his heart, Pope John Paul realized that the Eucharist is the greatest, most profound gift God has ever given us. The Eucharist contains everything the Church has to offer her people. Of course, that is Jesus Christ himself, who is our Savior and who gives himself to us in the living bread of the Eucharist.

John Paul wished to share this realization with everyone and to help invigorate among people what he referred to as a sense of "amazement" before the Eucharist. That's why he devoted so many of his writings to the topic.

In his encyclical *Ecclesia de Eucharistia* he taught

that those who feed on Christ in the Eucharist need not wait until the hereafter to receive eternal life: they already possess it on earth. He was saying that receiving the Eucharist gives us, even now, a taste of the fullness of life.

The Eucharist is a priceless treasure. But its simplicity—mere bread and wine—hides God's incredible holiness from our eyes and other senses. When we celebrate Eucharist we come in touch with our own creator and we grow in the divine life he shares with us.

Since Christ offers himself equally to everyone who comes forward to receive—poor and rich, young and old—the Eucharist is a sign of the great value that God places upon each person. So if we worship God in the Eucharist in the way we should, it has to make us become more and more aware of each person's dignity, no matter who they are or what they do.

"By grace you have been saved through faith, and this is not your own doing; it is the gift of God."

EPHESIANS 2:8

A PRAYER FROM THE HEART

O my beloved Jesus who has loved me so greatly, what more could you possibly do to make yourself loved by your people? If we really loved you, every church would be constantly filled with people thanking and worshiping you, burning with love for you, and gazing upon you with eyes of faith.

But instead, we tend to forget you and the love you have for us. We would never ignore anyone from whom we hope to obtain some little favor. Yet we leave you abandoned and alone. I wish that I could make up for all the neglect of others through my personal devotion to you.

I am sorry, Lord, that I have also been negligent of you and ungrateful for your presence in my life. I resolve from now on to change my attitude toward you by devoting all my activities to your service whenever I can.

Inflame me with your love so that I may live only to please you and love you. You deserve everyone's love. If there has ever been a time that I did not love you, I now ask forgiveness with a desire to do nothing else but love you forever.

O Jesus, you are my only good and my only lasting love. You are my all. Amen.

Uniting Past, Present, and Future

Every time we celebrate the Eucharist, we are spiritually brought back to the events of the very first paschal Triduum and those events are brought forward in time to us. In the Eucharist, Christ allows us to make his death and resurrection present at all times everywhere in the world. Part of God's mystery is that for God there is no time; there is no change; everything that happens, happens all at once. Through the Eucharist we enter into that mystery of eternity.

We know that Christ died for all of God's children. Every Mass offers the very same sacrifice to God the Father as Jesus offered on the cross two thousand years ago. That means that Christ's death and resurrection are still happening today—but on our altars, not on a cross. Jesus' gift of salvation becomes present to us "sacramentally" through all of history every time the Eucharist is celebrated.

Hence, the Eucharist we celebrate today is inseparable from the Lord's passion and is a sign of his death that is not confined to the past because Christ's works transcend all time. Jesus' words, "which is given for you" and "is poured out for you" (Luke 22:19, 20), indicate that Christ's sacrifice on the cross is present in the eucharistic banquet every time it is celebrated. Thus, we can be sure that at Mass, the Lord's death and resurrection—events that are central to our faith—truly become present once again.

So when we participate at Mass, Christ is continuing to procure our salvation for us. And in the Eucharist we help carry out Jesus' work of redeeming the whole world. That's an awesome responsibility! How could we ever pass up such an opportunity?

"Then he took a loaf of bread, and when he had given thanks, he broke it and gave it to them, saying, 'This is my body, which is given for you. Do this in remembrance of me.' And he did the same with the cup after supper, saying, 'This cup that is poured out for you is the new covenant in my blood.'"

LUKE 22:19–20

Prayer to Jesus in the Holy Eucharist

My Lord Jesus Christ, your presence on earth teaches me how to love others as you have loved me.

In your great love for me you continue to give yourself, body, blood, soul, and divinity in this sacrament of love.

As I pray here in your presence, enkindle in me the fire of your gospel. Nourish me with your love and compassion so that I may be your living presence to all I meet. Amen.

Uniting the Whole World

Pope John Paul II taught that since the Eucharist is universal, whenever it is celebrated in any one place it is also celebrated on every altar of the world at the same time. The Eucharist unites heaven and earth and touches all of creation. In one great act of praise, the Eucharist restores us and creation to our creator. Now redeemed, we are given back to God the Father.

One of the reasons the Holy Father loved the Mass so much is because Christ does more than give himself to us in the bread and wine. Christ's first gift is to the Father, then to us. And we offer ourselves to God in union with Christ. In its document on the Church, the bishops of Vatican Council II stated that we offer Christ—who is the divine victim—and ourselves to God (*Lumen Gentium*, 11).

In the Eucharist Christ gives back to the Father everything that he has received from him. We also need to honor our creator by offering in praise and thanksgiving all that we are and all that we have received.

*"That they may all be one. As you, Father, are in
me and I am in you, may they also be in us."*

JOHN 17:21

PRAYER OF SELF-OFFERING

Lord Jesus,
your gift of the Eucharist
strengthens me on the journey of life.
I want to offer you my entire being.
Transform me into your disciple and send me
   to those who are in need of your love.
May I become your hands for those
   who are helpless.
May I become your heart for those
   who are lonely.
Surround me, Lord, with your light and allow
   me to be an instrument of your peace and joy.

Uniting Us to Christ's Resurrection

The Eucharist is a sharing in Christ's resurrection since he has now become the "bread of life" (John 6:35). And Jesus promised that he would raise up anyone who partakes of his flesh and blood (see John 6:54). We can trust that promise because the Eucharist is the body of Christ now risen in glory. Whenever we eat the Eucharist we ingest the resurrection and hold it within ourselves. Thus, when we participate in the Eucharist, we receive—even here on earth—a foretaste of what we will have in heaven.

If we believe that is really true, then how could we ever stay away from the Eucharist?

"Those who eat my flesh and drink my blood have eternal life, and I will raise them up on the last day."

JOHN 6:54

A RESURRECTION PRAYER

Risen Jesus, fill me with the joy of your resurrection. Surround me with the radiant light of your glory. Transform all the areas of my life that are in need of your healing touch. Like Mary Magdalene, let me hear you whisper my name. Like the disciples on the road to Emmaus, help me to know you in the breaking of the bread, the holy Eucharist. With Saint Thomas, let me touch you and cry out, "My Lord and my God."

Risen Jesus, cover me with the radiance of your love. Let me be your messenger of peace, joy, and love to all I meet. Amen.

GRZEGORZ GALAZKA

Drawing Life From Eucharist

Vatican Council II taught that Eucharist is the source and summit of the Christian life (*Lumen Gentium*, 11). Pope John Paul II built on that theme as he taught that the Church was given birth in Christ's paschal mystery, and that it continues to draw its life from the Eucharist. He said that Eucharist is the central mystery around which the Church is built. Thus, the Eucharist is the heart of the Church's life.

Indeed, throughout the ages we all continue to draw life from Christ's redeeming sacrifice. Thus, we approach Eucharist not only as a remembrance of the Last Supper, but also to make actual contact with Christ since his sacrifice becomes present again and again on our altars, and is still being carried out every time the community gathers to celebrate Mass. Not only that, all people are invited to this sacrificial banquet so they may share in the life of Christ.

"Those who eat my flesh and drink my blood abide in me, and I in them. Just as the living Father sent me, and I live because of the Father, so whoever eats me will live because of me."

JOHN 6:56–57

PRAYER TO THE SOURCE OF OUR LIFE

O Lord, you have sent your Son to establish a new and perfect covenant with us, your people. It binds us to you intimately as your adopted children. Help us to remember that it was his body and blood that has redeemed us. May our sharing in the Eucharist be a sign of our belief in your promises, and may this sacrament be an everlasting source of life for us. Amen.

Forming Communion

The basic theology of Vatican Council II was an "ecclesiology of communion." That includes communion both with God and among people, and it happens especially through the Eucharist. In his encyclical titled *Church and Eucharist*, the Pope declared that the entire goal of the Eucharist is "communion of humankind with Christ and in him with the Father and the Holy Spirit" (22). Thus, Eucharist is appropriately called the sacrament of "communion."

It is around Christ in the Eucharist that the Church grows as a community. John Paul declared that "no Christian community can be built up unless it has its…center in the celebration of the most Holy Eucharist" (33). He referred to Saint John Chrysostom's image of bread made from many grains of wheat that bake into a single loaf. Each individual person is like a grain in the one bread of the Eucharist that transforms us into the one body of Christ (see homily on 1 Corinthians).

Our unity with one another in Christ's body helps fulfill our need for fraternity with our neighbors in the world. The eucharistic sacrifice is never a celebration of the local community alone. In the Eucharist each local parish community is a sign of the presence and unity of the whole Church. Therefore, no eucharistic community can ever be closed in upon itself but must always remain in harmony with all other local Catholic communities. In that way, through Sunday Mass, the Lord's day becomes also the Church's day, and that's how the Church serves as a sacrament of unity in the world.

"The grace of the Lord Jesus Christ, the love of God, and the communion of the Holy Spirit be with all of you."

2 CORINTHIANS 13:13

PRAYER AFTER COMMUNION
THE *ANIMA CHRISTI*

Soul of Christ, sanctify me.
Body of Christ, save me.
Blood of Christ, inebriate me.
Water from the side of Christ, wash me.
Passion of Christ, strengthen me.
O good Jesus, hear me.
Within your wounds hide me.
Never let me be separated from you.
From the evil one protect me.
At the hour of my death call me
and bid me come to you,
that with your saints I may praise you
forever and ever. Amen.

Sent As Missionaries

John Paul II observed that the mission of the Church continues the mission of Christ. We can understand more clearly our missionary role in the world when we gather around the altar as "Church" because at the end of every Mass each person is sent as a missionary "of the Eucharist" to bring to the whole world this great gift we have received.

After receiving the Eucharist, Christians (citizens of God's kingdom) are sent out to build a world in harmony with God's plan. Our whole lives must be totally committed to transforming the world. Indeed, anyone who truly encounters Christ in the Eucharist cannot help but proclaim God's merciful love through the way he or she lives.

The Pope emphasized that we draw spiritual energy from communion with Christ's body and blood. Each time we receive the sacrament our membership in the body of Christ is renewed. Then, through union with Christ, we are sent out as "the salt of the earth" and "the light of the world." We are sent because the whole purpose of Eucharist is to bring all people into communion with God.

"You are the salt of the earth;...You are the light of the world....Let your light shine before others, so that they may see your good works and give glory to your Father in heaven."

MATTHEW 5:13, 14, 16

PRAYER OF A MISSIONARY

O my God,
I wish to convert as many sinners
as there are grains of sand
in the sea and on the land,
as there are leaves on the trees,
blades of grass in the fields,
atoms in the air,
stars in the sky,
rays in the sun and moon,
creatures on the whole earth.
Amen.

Christus Remains Present Always

Close observers have reported that no pope ever spent as much time before the tabernacle as did John Paul II. The Holy Father knew well from personal experience that we must contemplate the face of Christ, and that this is best accomplished by eucharistic adoration that prolongs and increases the benefits of receiving holy Communion. It transforms the human heart because it foreshadows our eternal presence with God in heaven.

Eucharistic devotion outside of Mass is obviously linked to the sacramental celebration. The presence of Christ in the consecrated bread reserved in our churches and chapels points us toward communion with the Lord, both sacramentally and spiritually. The Mass is the most perfect prayer we can offer God. Yet by praying before Christ in the Eucharist—even apart from Mass—we can receive many graces. Saint Alphonsus Liguori, a doctor of the Church, believed that adoring Jesus in the Blessed Sacrament is the greatest of all devotions, just after reception of the sacraments.

Christian hope must shine forth throughout the world. For that reason, God has chosen to remain with us here on earth at all times in the Eucharist. Christ continues to walk beside us as our strength for the journey under the humble sign of bread changed into his body. Eucharistic devotion, therefore, is the worship of God's constant presence here on earth.

"And remember, I am with you always, to the end of the age."

MATTHEW 28:20

A SPIRITUAL COMMUNION BEFORE THE RESERVED EUCHARIST

My Jesus, I believe you are really here in the Blessed Sacrament. I love you more than anything in the world, and I hunger to receive your body and blood. But since I cannot receive Communion at this moment, feed my soul at least spiritually. I unite myself to you now as I do when I actually receive you. Never let me drift away from you. Amen.

Other Prayers
of Eucharistic Devotion

How to make a private holy hour before
the Blessed Sacrament

A eucharistic holy hour is nothing more—
and nothing less—than spending time in the
presence of Jesus in the holy Eucharist. People
commonly make a half-hour visit before the Blessed
Sacrament, whether exposed on the altar or reserved in the tabernacle. A holy hour may be observed in private or with a group.

Go to the area in which the Blessed Sacrament
is reserved. Kneel or be seated. Focus your atten-
tion on the presence of Jesus in the Eucharist. Greet
Jesus as you would a friend. Talk to him about what
is on your mind. Thank him for the ways you experience his presence in your life. Ask him for help in
the areas of your life in which you need assistance
and healing.

Recite a few prayers from a prayer book or read
a Scripture passage, either from the liturgy of the
day or a passage that is a favorite of yours. If a cer-

tain phrase, word, or image surfaces, stay with it and allow the Holy Spirit to lead your prayer.

If the Eucharist is exposed for adoration, allow yourself to gaze upon the consecrated host. This prayer of gazing is always a steppingstone to the prayer of contemplation. Silent meditation and quiet prayer before the Eucharist are the important elements of a holy hour.

Close your period of adoration by reciting the Lord's Prayer.

Visit to the Blessed Sacrament

SAINT ALPHONSUS LIGUORI

My Lord Jesus Christ, I believe that you are really here in this sacrament. Night and day you remain here compassionate and loving. You call, you wait for, you welcome, everyone who comes to visit you.

Unimportant though I am, I adore you. I thank you for all the wonderful graces you have given me. But I thank you especially for having given me yourself in this sacrament, for having asked your own Mother to mother me, for having called me here to talk to you.

I am here before you today to do three things: to thank you for these precious gifts, to make up for all the disrespect that you receive in this sacrament from those who offend you, to adore you everywhere in the world where you are present in this living bread but are left abandoned and unloved.

My Jesus, I love you with all my heart. I know I have displeased you often in the past—

I am sorry. With your help I promise never to do it again. I am only a miserable sinner, but I consecrate myself to you completely. I give you my will, my love, my desires, everything I own. From now on do what you please with me. All I ask is that you love me, that you keep me faithful to the end of my life. I ask for the grace to do your will exactly as you want it done.

I pray for the souls in purgatory—especially for those who were close to you in this sacrament and close to your Mother Mary. I pray for every soul hardened in sin. My Savior, I unite my love to the love of your divine heart, and I offer them both together to your Father. I beg him to accept this offering in your name. Amen.

A Prayer to Mary

Blessed Virgin Mary,
you were chosen by the Father
to be the mother of his Son,
our Lord Jesus Christ.
Your acceptance of the word Incarnate
brings joy to the whole Church
and salvation to the whole world.
Through your prayers
obtain for us a deeper love
for the mystery of the Eucharist.
May our devotion to the Lord Jesus Christ,
present in the sacrament of his love,
bring us one day to share in the
    heavenly banquet.
Mary, Mother of Christ, intercede for us.
Amen.

Pope John Paul II was deeply devoted to the Eucharist. It was the source and summit of his faith and his comfort in times of personal suffering. This collection of inspiring devotions invites everyone to explore the Eucharistic spirituality of the late Holy Father and to experience the profound joy that he found in an intimate relationship with our Lord.

Liguori
...URI DRIVE
...0 63057-9999

€ 1.15

Wendy Barnes
Cover image: Corbis

ISBN 0-7648-1421-4

50195>

9 780764 814211

11435